Explore new ideas!

Welcome to your California Reading/Writing Workshop

Read exciting literature, science and social studies texts!

Become an expert writer!

Build vocabulary and knowledge to unlock the Wonders of reading!

Use your student login to explore your interactive Reading/Writing Workshop, practice close reading, and more.

Go Digital! www.connected.mcgraw-hill.com

Cover and Title pages: Nathan Love

www.mheonline.com/readingwonders

Send all inquiries to:
McGraw-Hill Education
Two Penn Plaza
New York, New York 10121

ISBN: 978-0-02-131805-6
MHID: 0-02-131805-0

Printed in the United States of America.

3 4 5 6 7 8 9 LWI 20 19 18 17

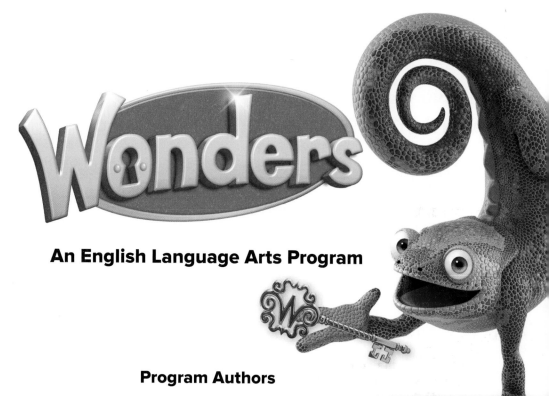

Wonders

An English Language Arts Program

Program Authors

Diane August

Donald R. Bear

Janice A. Dole

Jana Echevarria

Douglas Fisher

David Francis

Vicki Gibson

Jan Hasbrouck

Margaret Kilgo

Jay McTighe

Scott G. Paris

Timothy Shanahan

Josefina V. Tinajero

Mc
Graw
Hill
Education

Unit 2

Our Community

The Big Idea

What makes a community?   6

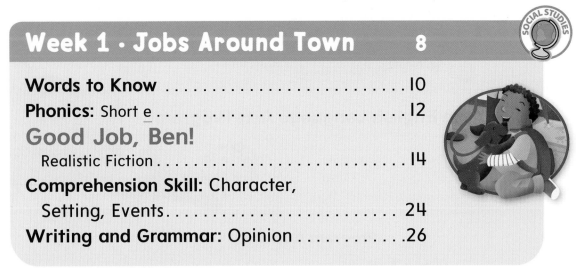

(t) Diane Greenseid; (c) Robin Boyer; (b) Amanda Gulliver

Go Digital! Find all lessons online at www.connected.mcgraw-hill.com

Week 3 · A Community in Nature 48

Week 4 · Let's Help 68

Week 5 · Follow the Map 88

Unit 2
Our Community

Diane Greenseid

On My Street

Houses standing in a row,
One of them is mine, I know.

Many families on one street,
Each with friends it's
fun to meet.

Everywhere I look I see,
This neighborhood is
home to me.

—Constance Andrea Keremes

The Big Idea

What makes a community?

Essential Question

What jobs need to be done in a community?

Go Digital!

At Work

COLLABORATE

Talk About It

How is this man's work important in the community?

Fuse/Getty Images

8   SL.1.1a See the California Standards section.

again

I may need to bake it **again.**

help

She will **help** find the street.

new

My class has a **new** teacher.

RF.1.3g, RF.1.3b See the California Standards section.

there

There is a lot of mail in his bag.

use

Use a scoop to pick up the rocks.

COLLABORATE

Your Turn

Say the sentence for each word. Then make up another sentence.

Go Digital! *Use the online visual glossary*

Short e

The letters e or ea can make the short e sound, as in **get** or **bread**.

men	vet	pet
bed	red	mess
head	well	dress
smell	deaf	bread

Robin Boyer

RF.1.3, RF.1.3b See the California Standards section.

Fred's pet hen can peck!

The top of its head is red.

Your Turn

Look for these words with the short e sound in "Good Job, Ben!"

Ben	head	get	yet
men	wet	step	bread
smells	ten	Jet	vet
well	pet	Glenn	read

Essential Question

What jobs need to be done in a community?

Read about jobs that people do around town.

Go Digital!

Robin Boyer

14

Good Job, Ben!

Ben and Mom head to town.
It is a big trip.
There is a lot to see.

Ben and Mom will get on the bus.
The driver stops on this block.

Good job!

Ben and Mom can not cross yet.
Stop! Stop! She can **help** them.

Big job!

Ben and Mom walk past.
Six men **use** a drill and fill cracks.
It will look **new** **again**.

Wet job!

Ben and Mom step in for bread.
Ben sniffs. It smells good.
Mom gets ten.

Hot job!

Ben and Mom get Jet.

Jet licks Ben.

The vet helped Jet get well quick.

Pet job!

Ben and Mom stop for books.
Ben can get help from Miss Glenn.

Glad job!

What did Ben get?
What has he read?
Ben read books on jobs.

Good job, Ben!

Character, Setting, Events

A **character** is a person or animal in a story.

The **setting** is where a story takes place.

The **events** are what happen in a story.

🔍 Find Text Evidence

Find the characters, the setting, and an event.

page 16

Ben and Mom head to town.
It is a big trip.
There is a lot to see.

Characters	Setting	Events
Ben Mom	at the bus stop	They are going to town.
Ben Mom	bakery	They buy bread.
Ben Mom	library	Ben finds books about jobs.

Your Turn

Talk about other characters, settings, and events in "Good Job, Ben!"

Go Digital! Use the interactive graphic organizer

Write About the Text

Pages 14–23

Eva

I answered the question: **Which hat in "Good Job, Ben!" do you think is the best for the worker's job?**

Student Model: *Opinion*

I think the six men's hats are the best for their job.

The men fix the street.

They wear hard, yellow hats.

Focus on an Idea
I wrote about the men's hats.

Clues
I used the picture to figure out a reason for my opinion.

Hard hats keep the men safe.
They guard the men's heads.
The hard hats are the best.

Grammar

Hats is an example of a **noun**.

Your Turn

Which job in "Good Job, Ben!" would you like to have? Why? Use text evidence to support your answer.

Go Digital!
Write your response online.
Use your editing checklist.

L.1.1b See the California Standards section.

27

Essential Question

What buildings do you know?
What are they made of?

Go Digital!

Sakis Papadopoulos/Robert Harding World Imagery/Getty Images

Our Town

COLLABORATE

Talk About It

What kinds of buildings are in this city?

29

could

They **could** build a house with logs.

live

Do you **live** in a tall building?

one

This hut has **one** room.

RF.1.3g See the California Standards section.

then

We open the door, and **then** we go out.

three

Three people can fit in a tent.

Your Turn

COLLABORATE

Say the sentence for each word. Then make up another sentence.

Go Digital! *Use the online visual glossary*

(tl) Image Source/Getty Images; (cl) Ben Bloom/Photodisc/Getty Images; (bl) MIXA/Getty Images; (tr) Kiyotaka Kitajima/amanaimages/Corbis; (br) imagebroker/Alamy

RF.1.3b See the California Standards section.

Short u

The letter u can make the short u sound in **hut**.

up   fun   but

bus   cup   duck

bug   drum   mud

tub   tucked   stuff

Amanda Gulliver

RF.1.3b, RF.1.3f See the California Standards section.

Buzz the bug can live in mud.

But can Buzz run and have fun?

Your Turn

Look for these words with short u in "Cubs in a Hut."

cubs	hut	Gus	mud
Russ	fun	Bud	up
rugs	stuff	us	snug
bugs	rug		

Essential Question

What buildings do you know? What are they made of?

Read about how three cubs build a hut.

Go Digital!

Amanda Gulliver

"Let's make a hut," said Gus.

"We **could** use mud," said Russ.

"It will be fun!" said Bud.

The cubs had a plan.
Bud got a big stack of sticks.
Russ and Gus got mud
and grass.

The cubs did a very good job.

"Let's move in!" yelled Russ.

"Yes, yes!" yelled Bud and Gus.

The cubs set up rugs and beds.
They filled up the hut with lots
of stuff.

Then **one** night **three** cubs got up.

Drip, drip, drip!

"My bed is wet!" yelled Bud.

"My head is wet!" yelled Gus.

"It's not fun to **live** in a wet hut!" yelled Russ.

"We must fix it," said Bud.

"It will not drip on us," said Gus.

"We will not get wet," said Russ.

Amanda Gulliver

It is good to live in a dry hut.
Three cubs are as snug as bugs
in a rug!

Character, Setting, Events

A character is a person or animal in a story.

The setting is where a story takes place.

The events are what happen in a story.

🔍 Find Text Evidence

Use the words and the pictures to find a character, setting, and event in the story.

page 37

The cubs had a plan.
Bud got a big stack of sticks.
Russ and Gus got mud
and grass.

Amanda Gulliver

Character	Setting	Events
Bud	forest	He got sticks.
Russ	forest	He got mud.
Gus	forest	He got grass.

Your Turn

Talk about the characters, setting, and events in "Cubs in a Hut."

Go Digital! *Use the interactive graphic organizer*

45

Pages 34–43

Write About the Text

Luis

I responded to the prompt: **What do the cubs do first, next, and last to fix the roof of their hut?**

Student Model: *Informative Text*

The cubs must fix the roof.

First, the cubs get nails.

Then, they get wood.

Next, they find a ladder.

Beginning Sentence
I wrote a beginning that names the topic.

Clues
I used the picture to figure out what the cubs do.

W.1.2 See the California Standards section.

Then, they go up to the roof.

Last, they pound the nails.

Now the roof is fixed!

Grammar

The **singular noun** and **plural noun** are used correctly.

COLLABORATE

Your Turn

Look at pages 36 through 39. What plans did the bears use for building their hut? Write the directions they followed. Use details from the story in your answer.

Go Digital!
Write your response online.
Use your editing checklist.

Amanda Gulliver

Essential Question

Where do animals live together?

Go Digital!

Peter Scoones/Taxi/Getty Images

SL.1.1a See the California Standards section.

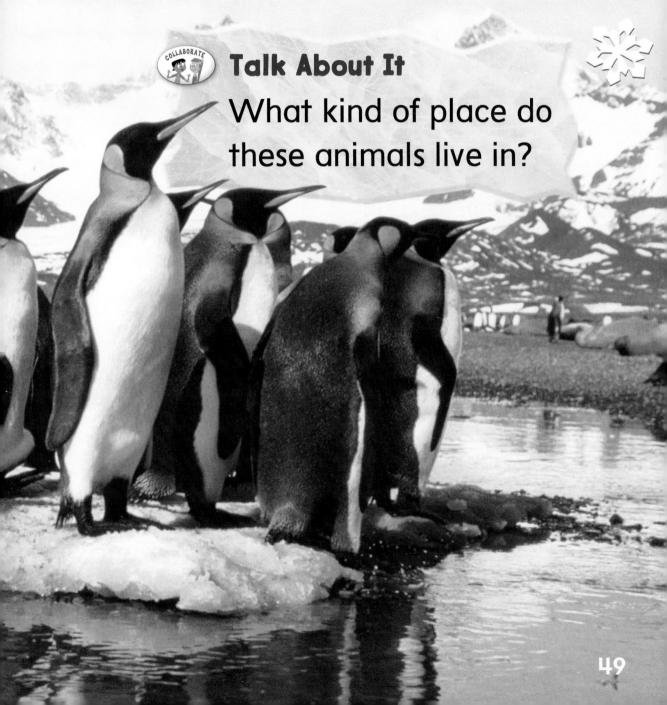

Animals at Home

Talk About It

What kind of place do these animals live in?

eat

Chipmunks like to **eat** nuts.

no

A snake has **no** legs.

of

The birds sit in a nest **of** twigs.

under

They dive down **under** the water.

who

Who can see the bug?

COLLABORATE

Your Turn

Say the sentence for each word. Then make up another sentence.

Go Digital! Use the online visual glossary

End Blends

The letters nd, nk, nt, sk, st, and mp together make the ending sounds in **land**, **drink**, **went**, **ask**, **rest**, and **damp**.

and	**fast**	**jump**
send	**desk**	**must**
hunt	**mask**	**plant**
skunk	**trunk**	**stamp**

Margie Moore

The sku<u>nk</u> is plu<u>mp</u> <u>an</u>d fa<u>st</u>!

It will play <u>an</u>d hu<u>nt</u>.

Your Turn

COLLABORATE

Look for these words with end blends in "The Best Spot."

be<u>st</u>	pla<u>nts</u>	ne<u>st</u>
tru<u>nk</u>	a<u>nts</u>	a<u>nd</u>
re<u>st</u>	sa<u>nd</u>	stu<u>mp</u>
ju<u>mp</u>	mu<u>st</u>	hu<u>nts</u>
du<u>sk</u>	we<u>nt</u>	sku<u>nk</u>

Essential Question

Where do animals live together?

Read about the animals in a forest.

Go Digital!

The Best Spot

Purestock/Getty Images; (border) Carl Keyes/Alamy

This is a forest.

This spot has lots **of** animals.

Deer live here. They **eat** plants.

But **who** is in the grass?

A rabbit's head pops up!

What is up there?

Look up, up, up.

It is a nest.

The mom gets big bugs. Yum!

What is on the trunk?

It is a nest, too.

Lots of wasps live in it.

Ants live here, too.

Ants pick up twigs and grass.

Ants zip in and out.

Ants have **no** rest!

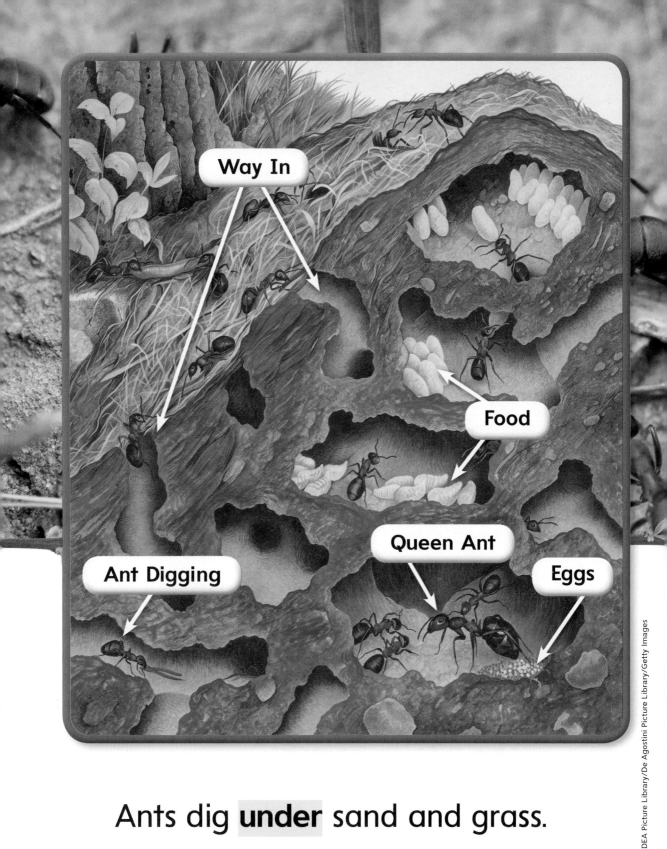

Way In

Food

Ant Digging

Queen Ant

Eggs

Ants dig **under** sand and grass.

Fox kits hop on a stump.

Mom fox lets the kits run and jump.

The kits must eat.

Dad fox hunts at dusk.

Who went hunting, too?
A skunk!

This spot has lots of animals!

Main Topic and Key Details

The **main topic** is what the selection is about.

Key details give information about the main topic.

 Find Text Evidence

The selection is about a place where animals live together.

Find a detail about one of the animals.

page 56

This is a forest.

This spot has lots **of** animals.

Deer live here. They **eat** plants.

RI.1.2 See the California Standards section.

Purestock/Getty Images

Main Topic		
Lots of animals live in the forest.		
Detail	**Detail**	**Detail**
Deer live in the forest. They eat plants.	Ants make their home under the ground.	Some forest animals hunt at night.

Your Turn

COLLABORATE

Talk about the main topic and other details in "The Best Spot."

Go Digital! *Use the interactive graphic organizer*

Zoonar GmbH/Alamy

The Best Spot

Pages 54–63

Write About the Text

Ben

I responded to the prompt: **Write two pages of an informative text about animals that live in the sea.**

Student Model: *Informative Text*

Main Idea
My first two sentences are about my main idea.

Facts
I included facts to tell about the sea.

This is a sea.

This spot has lots of animals.

Sharks live here.

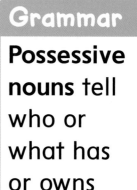

Sharks eat fish.

But who is behind a rock?

A turtle's head pops out!

Grammar

Possessive nouns tell who or what has or owns something. **Turtle's** is a possessive noun.

COLLABORATE

Your Turn

Use "The Best Spot" as a model and write the first two pages of an informative text about animals that live in a park.

Go Digital!
Write your response online.
Use your editing checklist.

L.1.1b See the California Standards section.

Essential Question

How do people help out in the community?

Go Digital!

Make It Better

COLLABORATE

Talk About It

What are these children doing together to make a difference?

all

Let's pick up **all** the trash.

call

Who will you **call** to help?

day

It is a good **day** to plant.

her

Mom recycles **her** bottles.

want

I **want** to help my Gram.

Your Turn

COLLABORATE

Say the sentence for each word. Then make up another sentence.

Go Digital! Use the online visual glossary

th, sh, -ng

The letters th make the sound you hear in **that** or **path**.

The letters sh make the sound you hear in **shop** or **fish**.

The letters -ng make the sound you hear in **ring**.

then	shut	wing
math	thank	hang
shed	sing	crash
with	fresh	sting

Sergio DeGiorgi

RF.1.3a See the California Standards section.

I ba<u>ng</u> my drum on <u>th</u>is <u>sh</u>ip.

Can Be<u>th</u> si<u>ng</u> a so<u>ng</u>?

Your Turn

Look for these words with <u>th</u>, <u>sh</u>, and -<u>ng</u> in "Thump Thump Helps Out."

<u>th</u>ump	<u>th</u>umped	sa<u>ng</u>
hu<u>sh</u>	<u>th</u>at	ba<u>ng</u>
cra<u>sh</u>	wi<u>sh</u>	<u>Sh</u>eldon
<u>th</u>ink	ru<u>sh</u>ed	lo<u>ng</u>
wi<u>th</u>	so<u>ng</u>	bri<u>ng</u>s	<u>th</u>is

Genre Fantasy

Essential Question

How do people help out in the community?

Go Digital!

Sergio DeGiorgi

Thump Thump Helps Out

Thump Thump liked to thump.

He thumped a lot as he sang.

He thumped a lot just for fun.

"Hush! Stop that, Thump Thump!"
yelled **all** the little rabbits.

"We do not like it one bit!"

But Thump Thump did not stop.

One **day**, there was a problem.

Thump Thump's bus hit a rock.

Bang! Crash! Clunk!

His bus got stuck in the mud.

The little rabbits could not fix it.

Sergio DeGiorgi

"We wish big rabbits could get us home," sniffed the little rabbits.

"Help us!" yelled Miss Sheldon.

But not one big rabbit heard her call.

Thump Thump had a plan.

"I think I can help," he sang.

He thumped and thumped and thumped.

Big rabbits all over heard
Thump Thump's thump.

They rushed to help fix the bus.

The kids got home fast.

Sergio DeGiorgi

"Thump Thump, can you help us?" asked the big rabbits.

"We **want** you to thump loud and long if a rabbit needs help."

"Thump, Thump!" went Thump
Thump, with a song.

And Thump Thump thumps and
brings help to this day.

Character, Setting, Events

A **character** is a person or animal in a story.

The **setting** is where a story takes place.

The **events** are what happen in a story.

 Find Text Evidence

Use the words and pictures to find the events that happen in the story.

page 76

Thump Thump liked to thump.

He thumped a lot as he sang.

He thumped a lot just for fun.

Sergio DeGiorgi

84 RL.1.3, RL.1.7 See the California Standards section.

Characters	Setting	Events
Thump Thump	forest	He thumped his feet a lot.
Rabbits	forest	The bus hit a rock and got stuck in the mud.
Thump Thump	forest	He thumped his feet to get help.

Your Turn

COLLABORATE

Talk about the characters, setting, and events in "Thump Thump Helps Out."

Go Digital! Use the interactive graphic organizer

85

Pages 74–83

Write About the Text

Robert

I responded to the prompt: **Write a fantasy about a helpful character. Use "Thump Thump" as a model.**

Student Model: *Narrative Text*

Chip Chipmunk likes to run.

He runs up and down trees.

He runs quickly in the park.

One day Chip passes Dad.

Chip's Grandma is sick.

Chip's Dad has nuts for her.

Beginning
My story has a beginning.

Grammar

A **proper noun,** such as **Chip,** begins with a capital letter.

"Could I help you, Dad?"

Chip asks.

"I can run the nuts to Grandma's house."

Chip is so helpful!

Characters
I made the animals talk like in the story.

COLLABORATE

Your Turn

Use "Thump Thump Helps Out" as a model to write a fantasy about a character who has an unusual habit.

Go Digital!
Write your response online.
Use your editing checklist.

Essential Question

How can you find your way around?

Go Digital!

SL.1.1a See the California Standards section.

Jeff Greenberg/Alamy

Map It!

COLLABORATE

Talk About It

What is the family using to get directions?

around

I like to ride **around** the park.

by

The bus stops **by** my house.

many

There are **many** shops in town.

RF.1.3b, RF.1.3g See the California Standards section.

place

Let's look for this **place** on a map.

walk

We **walk** to the library.

Your Turn

COLLABORATE

Say the sentence for each word. Then make up another sentence.

Go Digital! **Use the online visual glossary**

ch, -tch, wh, ph

The letters ch and -tch make the sound you hear in **chop** and **catch**.

The letters wh make the sound you hear in **when**.

The letters ph make the sound you hear in **Phil**.

inch	whiz	chat
itch	when	graph
lunch	check	stitch
which	sketch	much

Phil will sketch a graph for math.

When will he get his lunch?

Your Turn

Look for these words with ch, -tch, wh, and ph in "Which Way on the Map?"

which	Mitch	Steph
children	chat	benches
catch	such	lunch check

Essential Question

How can you find your way around?

Read about places in a town.

Go Digital!

Lane Oatey/Getty Images

Which Way on the Map?

Mitch and Steph live in a big town.

There is a lot to see.

Let's **walk around** with them.

This is the town on a map.

It shows each **place** in town.

This place has red bricks.

Many children go here.

Mitch and Steph go here, too.

Which place is this?

Can you spot it on the map?

This place is **by** a lake. People chat on benches. Mitch and Steph will run and play catch. It is such fun!

Which place is this?

Can you spot it on the map?

This place has a big box. Mitch and Steph stop and get stamps. They drop a letter in the big box. Which place is this?

Can you spot it on the map?

Where can Mitch and
Steph get lunch?

Check the map!

Main Topic and Key Details

The **main topic** is what the selection is about.

Key details give information about the main topic.

 Find Text Evidence

The selection is about how to use a map.

Find a detail about the school in Mitch and Steph's town.

page 98

This place has red bricks.

Main Topic		
How to Use a Map to Find Places in Town		
Detail	**Detail**	**Detail**
The school has red bricks. The school is on the map.	The playground is by the lake. The playground is on the map.	The post office has a big box. The post office is on the map.

Your Turn

COLLABORATE

Talk about the main topic and details in "Which Way on the Map?"

Go Digital! *Use the interactive graphic organizer*

Writing and Grammar

Write About the Text

Pages 94–103

Maria

I answered the question: **Which of the map features help Mitch and Steph get around town?**

Student Model: *Informative Text*

The pictures and signs on the map help Mitch and Steph. Mitch and Steph look at the pictures on the map. The pictures look like places in town.

Clues

I used pictures from the maps to help me answer the question.

Tetra Images/Getty Images

106 W.1.2 See the California Standards section.

Read
Together

Supporting Details
I included details about signs.

Grammar

The word **children** is an **irregular plural noun.** It means more than one child.

The signs tell them the names of the places.
The children can tell where they are using the pictures and words.

COLLABORATE

Your Turn

Why does the author use photographs and parts of the map? What does this help a reader to understand? Use text evidence to support your answer.

Go Digital!
Write your response online.
Use your editing checklist.

DAJ/Getty Images

California Common Core State Standards

At the bottom of some pages in this book, you will see letters and numbers. What do these numbers and letters mean? In **RL.1.1**, **RL** stands for **R**eading Standards for **L**iterature. The number **1** stands for Grade **1**. The number **1** is the standard number.

Subject Area	Grade Level	Standard Number
RL	1	1

This California standard is about being able to ask questions and give answers based on information in the text to show what you have learned.

1. Ask and answer such questions as *who, what, where, when, why,* and *how* to demonstrate understanding of key details in a text.

This means that you will learn to ask questions to find out the information you need from a story. You will learn to understand what the author says directly in the text. You will also learn to find deeper meaning in the text by using details and clues. The author put these clues into the story. It is the reader's job to figure them out!

The Grade 1 California Standards for Reading and Language Arts have six subject areas.

RL = Reading Standards for Literature

RI = Reading Standards for Informational Text

RF = Reading Standards for Foundational Skills

W = Writing Standards

SL = Speaking and Listening Standards

L = Language Standards

Your standards in all of these subject areas follow. **Take a look!**

English Language Arts & Literacy in History/ Social Studies, Science, and Technical Subjects

Grade 1

Reading Standards for Literature	
Key Ideas and Details	
RL.1.1	Ask and answer questions about key details in a text.
RL.1.2	Retell stories, including key details, and demonstrate understanding of their central message or lesson.
RL.1.3	Describe characters, settings, and major events in a story, using key details.
Craft and Structure	
RL.1.4	Identify words and phrases in stories or poems that suggest feelings or appeal to the senses. (See grade 1 Language standards 4–6 for additional expectations.) CA
RL.1.5	Explain major differences between books that tell stories and books that give information, drawing on a wide reading of a range of text types.
RL.1.6	Identify who is telling the story at various points in a text.
Integration of Knowledge and Ideas	
RL.1.7	Use illustrations and details in a story to describe its characters, setting, or events.
RL.1.8	(Not applicable to literature)
RL.1.9	Compare and contrast the adventures and experiences of characters in stories.
Range of Reading and Level of Text Complexity	
RL.1.10	With prompting and support, read prose and poetry of appropriate complexity for grade 1.
RL.1.10a	Activate prior knowledge related to the information and events in a text. CA
RL.1.10b	Confirm predictions about what will happen next in a text. CA

Reading Standards for Informational Text

Key Ideas and Details

RI.1.1   Ask and answer questions about key details in a text.

RI.1.2   Identify the main topic and retell key details of a text.

RI.1.3   Describe the connection between two individuals, events, ideas, or pieces of information in a text.

Craft and Structure

RI.1.4   Ask and answer questions to help determine or clarify the meaning of words and phrases in a text. (See grade 1 Language standards 4–6 for additional expectations.) CA

RI.1.5   Know and use various text structures (e.g., sequence) and text features (e.g., headings, tables of contents, glossaries, electronic menus, icons) to locate key facts or information in a text. CA

RI.1.6   Distinguish between information provided by pictures or other illustrations and information provided by the words in a text.

Integration of Knowledge and Ideas

RI.1.7   Use the illustrations and details in a text to describe its key ideas.

RI.1.8   Identify the reasons an author gives to support points in a text.

RI.1.9   Identify basic similarities in and differences between two texts on the same topic (e.g., in illustrations, descriptions, or procedures).

Range of Reading and Level of Text Complexity

RI.1.10   With prompting and support, read informational texts appropriately complex for grade 1.

RI.1.10a   Activate prior knowledge related to the information and events in a text. CA

RI.1.10b   Confirm predictions about what will happen next in a text. CA

Grade 1

Reading Standards for Foundational Skills

Print Concepts

RF.1.1	Demonstrate understanding of the organization and basic features of print.
RF.1.1a	Recognize the distinguishing features of a sentence (e.g., first word, capitalization, ending punctuation).

Phonological Awareness

RF.1.2	Demonstrate understanding of spoken words, syllables, and sounds (phonemes).
RF.1.2a	Distinguish long from short vowel sounds in spoken single-syllable words.
RF.1.2b	Orally produce single-syllable words by blending sounds (phonemes), including consonant blends.
RF.1.2c	Isolate and pronounce initial, medial vowel, and final sounds (phonemes) in spoken single-syllable words.
RF.1.2d	Segment spoken single-syllable words into their complete sequence of individual sounds (phonemes).

Phonics and Word Recognition

RF.1.3	Know and apply grade-level phonics and word analysis skills in decoding words both in isolation and in text. CA
RF.1.3a	Know the spelling-sound correspondences for common consonant digraphs.
RF.1.3b	Decode regularly spelled one-syllable words.
RF.1.3c	Know final -e and common vowel team conventions for representing long vowel sounds.
RF.1.3d	Use knowledge that every syllable must have a vowel sound to determine the number of syllables in a printed word.
RF.1.3e	Decode two-syllable words following basic patterns by breaking the words into syllables.
RF.1.3f	Read words with inflectional endings.
RF.1.3g	Recognize and read grade-appropriate irregularly spelled words.

Fluency	
RF.1.4	Read with sufficient accuracy and fluency to support comprehension.
RF.1.4a	Read on-level text with purpose and understanding.
RF.1.4b	Read on-level text orally with accuracy, appropriate rate, and expression on successive readings.
RF.1.4c	Use context to confirm or self-correct word recognition and understanding, rereading as necessary.

Writing Standards

Text Types and Purposes

W.1.1	Write opinion pieces in which they introduce the topic or name the book they are writing about, state an opinion, supply a reason for the opinion, and provide some sense of closure.
W.1.2	Write informative/explanatory texts in which they name a topic, supply some facts about the topic, and provide some sense of closure.
W.1.3	Write narratives in which they recount two or more appropriately sequenced events, include some details regarding what happened, use temporal words to signal event order, and provide some sense of closure.

Production and Distribution of Writing

W.1.4	(Begins in grade 2) CA
W.1.5	With guidance and support from adults, focus on a topic, respond to questions and suggestions from peers, and add details to strengthen writing as needed.
W.1.6	With guidance and support from adults, use a variety of digital tools to produce and publish writing, including in collaboration with peers.

Research to Build and Present Knowledge

W.1.7	Participate in shared research and writing projects (e.g., explore a number of "how-to" books on a given topic and use them to write a sequence of instructions).
W.1.8	With guidance and support from adults, recall information from experiences or gather information from provided sources to answer a question.
W.1.9	(Begins in grade 4)

Range of Writing

W.1.10	(Begins in grade 2) CA

Speaking and Listening Standards

Comprehension and Collaboration

SL.1.1	Participate in collaborative conversations with diverse partners about *grade 1 topics and texts* with peers and adults in small and larger groups.
SL.1.1a	Follow agreed-upon rules for discussions (e.g., listening to others with care, speaking one at a time about the topics and texts under discussion).
SL.1.1b	Build on others' talk in conversations by responding to the comments of others through multiple exchanges.
SL.1.1c	Ask questions to clear up any confusion about the topics and texts under discussion.
SL.1.2	Ask and answer questions about key details in a text read aloud or information presented orally or through other media.
SL.1.2a	Give, restate, and follow simple two-step directions. CA
SL.1.3	Ask and answer questions about what a speaker says in order to gather additional information or clarify something that is not understood.

Presentation of Knowledge and Ideas

SL.1.4	Describe people, places, things, and events with relevant details, expressing ideas and feelings clearly.
SL.1.4a	Memorize and recite poems, rhymes, and songs with expression. CA
SL.1.5	Add drawings or other visual displays to descriptions when appropriate to clarify ideas, thoughts, and feelings.
SL.1.6	Produce complete sentences when appropriate to task and situation. (See grade 1 Language standards 1 and 3 for specific expectations.)

Language Standards

Conventions of Standard English

L.1.1	Demonstrate command of the conventions of standard English grammar and usage when writing or speaking.
L.1.1a	Print all upper- and lowercase letters.
L.1.1b	Use common, proper, and possessive nouns.
L.1.1c	Use singular and plural nouns with matching verbs in basic sentences (e.g., *He hops; We hop*).
L.1.1d	Use personal (subject, object), possessive, and indefinite pronouns (e.g., *I, me, my; they, them, their; anyone, everything*). CA
L.1.1e	Use verbs to convey a sense of past, present, and future (e.g., *Yesterday I walked home; Today I walk home; Tomorrow I will walk home*).
L.1.1f	Use frequently occurring adjectives.
L.1.1g	Use frequently occurring conjunctions (e.g., *and, but, or, so, because*).
L.1.1h	Use determiners (e.g., articles, demonstratives).
L.1.1i	Use frequently occurring prepositions (e.g., *during, beyond, toward*).
L.1.1j	Produce and expand complete simple and compound declarative, interrogative, imperative, and exclamatory sentences in response to prompts.
L.1.2	Demonstrate command of the conventions of standard English capitalization, punctuation, and spelling when writing.
L.1.2a	Capitalize dates and names of people.
L.1.2b	Use end punctuation for sentences.
L.1.2c	Use commas in dates and to separate single words in a series.
L.1.2d	Use conventional spelling for words with common spelling patterns and for frequently occurring irregular words.
L.1.2e	Spell untaught words phonetically, drawing on phonemic awareness and spelling conventions.

Knowledge of Language

L.1.3	(Begins in grade 2)

Grade 1 · Language Standards (continued)

Vocabulary Acquisition and Use	
L.1.4	Determine or clarify the meaning of unknown and multiple-meaning words and phrases based on *grade 1 reading and content,* choosing flexibly from an array of strategies.
L.1.4a	Use sentence-level context as a clue to the meaning of a word or phrase.
L.1.4b	Use frequently occurring affixes as a clue to the meaning of a word.
L.1.4c	Identify frequently occurring root words (e.g., *look*) and their inflectional forms (e.g., *looks, looked, looking*).
L.1.5	With guidance and support from adults, demonstrate understanding of word relationships and nuances in word meanings.
L.1.5a	Sort words into categories (e.g., colors, clothing) to gain a sense of the concepts the categories represent.
L.1.5b	Define words by category and by one or more key attributes (e.g., a *duck* is a bird that swims; a *tiger* is a large cat with stripes).
L.1.5c	Identify real-life connections between words and their use (e.g., note places at home that are *cozy*).
L.1.5d	Distinguish shades of meaning among verbs differing in manner (e.g., *look, peek, glance, stare, glare, scowl*) and adjectives differing in intensity (e.g., *large, gigantic*) by defining or choosing them or by acting out the meanings.
L.1.6	Use words and phrases acquired through conversations, reading and being read to, and responding to texts, including using frequently occurring conjunctions to signal simple relationships (e.g., *because*).